ideals®
FRIENDSHIP

50 Years of Celebrating Life's Most Treasured Moments

Vol. 51, No. 6

"The only way to have a friend is to be one."
Ralph Waldo Emerson

IDEALS—Vol. 51, No. 6 September MCMXCIV IDEALS (ISSN 0019-137X) is published eight times a year: February, March, May, June, August, September, November, December by IDEALS PUBLICATIONS INCORPORATED, 565 Marriott Drive, Suite 800, Nashville, TN 37214. Second-class postage paid at Nashville, Tennessee, and additional mailing offices. Copyright © MCMXCIV by IDEALS PUBLICATIONS INCORPORATED. POSTMASTER: Send address changes to Ideals, PO Box 148000, Nashville, TN 37214-8000. All rights reserved. Title IDEALS registered U.S. Patent Office.
SINGLE ISSUE—$4.95
ONE-YEAR SUBSCRIPTION—eight consecutive issues as published—$19.95
TWO-YEAR SUBSCRIPTION—sixteen consecutive issues as published—$35.95
Outside U.S.A., add $6.00 per subscription year for postage and handling.

Printed and bound in USA by The Banta Company, Menasha, Wisconsin.

Printed on Weyerhaeuser Husky.

The paper used in this publication meets the minimum requirements of American National Standard for Information Sciences—Permanence of Paper for Printed Library Materials, ANSI Z39.48-1984.

Unsolicited manuscripts will not be returned without a self-addressed, stamped envelope.

ISBN 0-8249-1120-2

Cover Photo, BUCKET OF ZINNIAS, Norman Poole Photography

Inside Front Cover, RUBY TREE, Original watercolor by David Lenz

Inside Back Cover, WELCOME, Original watercolor by David Lenz

In Autumn

Elisabeth Weaver Winstead

In autumn's breeze, leaves tumble down,
Vermillion, crimson, bronze, and brown.
The shim'ring oaks along the lane
Wear rainbow halos once again.

Bright bittersweet and woodbine twine;
Ripe grapes hang purpling on the vine;
Broad orchard trees stand bare and clean,
Their outstretched boughs no longer green.

Against the arching blue-hazed sky
The smoke-curled wreaths of bonfires fly.
Brown nuts drop to the leaf-strewn ground,
Where orange pumpkins now abound.

Flocks of geese in V-formation
Soar to a sun-warmed destination;
Full harvest moon-gold glazes all;
Night echoes crickets' farewell call.

AUTUMN LANE
Sugar Hill, New Hampshire
William H. Johnson
Johnson's Photography

Bittersweet

Merle Hazard

Untamed, the bittersweet spreads out
Along my wooden fence
In careless disarray; I doubt
That it has any sense

Of just how flagrant a display
Its bright red berries give
To autumn's somber, fading day.
How dare this wanton live!

In luscious splendor does it grow,
So heedless to conform
To rules of formal gardens; it
Just disregards the norm.

The viney statement that it makes
Speaks to my gardener's eye
Of life lived only for its sake
And never asking why.

Yet pause I must to contemplate
The message that it brings
Of wisdom, natural, innate,
The trust from which it springs.

So grow, red-berried vine, grow on,
Your promise so intense;
Grow on, red-berried vine, grow on
And pique my waking sense.

Autumn . . . season of mist and mellow fruitfulness.

—John Keats

This Page
BITTERSWEET BERRIES
Floyd Knobs, Indiana
Dan Dempster Photography

Opposite Page
CLIMBING BITTERSWEET
William H. Johnson
Johnson's Photography

4

September Gardens

Patience Strong

Lovely is the garden now in this its crowning hour,
Lovely with the final flush of shrub and fruit and flower.
Apples blush a rosy red, and loaded branches bend
In the good and golden month that comes at summer's end.

Blue hydrangeas, rainbow asters, mauve petunias,
Marigolds and gladioli, sunflowers, dahlias,
Glory of chrysanthemums, bronze, amber, and maroon,
White and crimson roses stir my memories of June.

Could I call a halt to time for just an hour or so,
This the moment I would choose, before the swallows go,
When the garden wears its brightest colors, rich and bold,
And the summer's loveliness is touched with autumn gold.

Country
CHRONICLE
Lansing Christman

I have again taken up my country walks. Those torrid days back in the summer were not conducive to my well-being. Some indoor walkers suggested that I start walking in the air-conditioned recreation areas or even in the malls during the hot summer days. There are reasons why I chose not to heed their well-intended advice.

When I walk, I want the land around me, land with its fields and orchards, the pastures with their cows and horses. I want to see and hear the birds. I want to see the flowers and brushlands, the woodland trees, the grasses and clover.

It is mid-September, and I again put on my walking shoes. For the most part, there is a gradual cooling of temperatures, a soft touch of crispness in the air. Yet, even in September, there are already signs of the maturing year: the gold of the goldenrod by the roadsides, the gray plumes of the wild clematis over the thickets by the brook. Woodbine, with its deep red leaves, is climbing the trees as though it is in a hurry to start the colorful parade along the roadside and woodlands. Sumac leaves display their colorful autumnal garb of scarlet and red.

I am well aware that in the season to come, when winter's cold nips at my face and hands and keen damp winds chill me to the bone, I may have to curtail my walks again. There will be times when I will be forced to stay indoors, enjoying the comfort of heated rooms, but until then I will walk. I will be out every day I can to enjoy the art of walking. I may see the crows struggling against the wind as they fly overhead. I may see the hawks gliding with a few wing beats, keeping a sharp lookout on the land below. I too keep a sharp lookout for the regal beauty of the countryside and God's gift in the glory of nature, so appealing and comforting to one who is a part of the Blue Ridge foothills.

The author of two published books, Lansing Christman has been contributing to Ideals *for over twenty years. Mr. Christman has also been published in several American, foreign, and braille anthologies. He lives in rural South Carolina.*

UNICOI MOUNTAINS
Cherokee National Forest, Tennessee
Jeff Gnass Photography

September Days

LaVerne P. Larson

The sky is like a sea of blue
With just a white cloud ship or two.
The sun shines from its lofty tower
With beams much like a golden shower.

Sweet notes of birds float on the air;
September days are cool and fair.
The grass and leaves persist in green,
Clinging to a summer scene.

And now and then a butterfly
Appears and gayly hurries by.
The locusts sing, the crickets too,
For days like this will soon be few.

A changing scene will then appear
As Autumn's cloak spreads far and near,
And then King Winter's gown of white
Will bid sweet Autumn to take flight.

September is the in-between
When Summer is no longer queen;
And as these lovely days depart,
They will leave memories for your heart.

Memories of a Grade School Teacher

Gladys Bussey

I began teaching in Oklahoma in 1935. Times were tough during the Great Depression, and school districts were often hard pressed to pay teachers, let alone purchase books or supplies. My beginning salary was sixty dollars per month, but there was no guarantee that I'd be able to cash the warrant or be paid for a nine-month term.

My first year I taught grades four and five and coached boys' basketball. I had never even seen a basketball game, so I just acted as a referee to settle arguments on the court. The next year I was assigned to teach first and second grades, but I had no books for first grade. I found a large chart with *The Gingerbread Man,* so I taught them to read, "I am a gingerbread boy, I am, I am. I can run, I can, I can." After the students learned that, I made up my own stories.

I also had composed my own spelling list and taught the students the sounds of the letters. When the county superintendent came to observe my teaching at the end of the year, he said I was teaching phonics, so I must be a good teacher. I was rehired.

When I taught third grade, the state course of study for that year required a six-week unit on American Indians. Since the Indians were not mentioned in the books, it was up to me to furnish the material. I read everything I could find about Indians. Applying what I taught them, the children wrote stories about Indian customs and daily living skills and illustrated their stories with their own drawings. In the classroom we built a tepee with a long pole and brown paper. We learned Indian songs and dances and concluded our study with an Indian play. The children turned brown grocery sacks into painted Indian vests for costumes.

In those days, grade school teachers taught everything, even art, music, and physical education. We also performed as dentists by pulling baby teeth, barbers by trimming bangs, nurses by bandaging skinned knees, and counselors by listening to troubled hearts. I taught school for thirty-eight years, and I still thrill to see the sparkle in a child's eye as he learns.

One of my happiest memories came the year I retired. A small boy, with tears in his eyes, put his arms around me and said, "I'm sure gonna miss you. You're just like my grandma." I thought I'd be relieved when my last day of teaching came, but when I handed in my key, I went away with a lump in my throat and tears in my eyes.

SCHOOL DAYS
Original painting by George Hinke

Autumn Magic

Kenneth D. Loss

There is magic every autumn
   'Ere the leaves come floating down,
As they dye their summer wardrobes
   Shades of yellow, gold, and brown.

Every tree is splashed with color,
   And the sky is changing too,
As the songbirds seek warm climates
   Where they'll live the winter through.

Mother Nature's very busy
   Putting Summertime to bed

'Neath a counterpane of rainbows
   Covered by a cotton spread.

Yes, the magic of each autumn
   Is a sign of rest to come
For the millions of God's creatures
   And the good earth they are from.

So enjoy the end of summer
   And the dream of winter fun
As you live that special season
   When Fall's magic work is done.

From My Garden Journal

by Deana Deck

PEONIES

If a competition should ever be held in my garden for the title of Friendship Flower, the peony would be the leading candidate. My friends know that I keep a garden because I love a riot of colorful blooms outdoors and vases full of bright blossoms indoors. Nothing pleases me as much as a spectacular display of big gorgeous flowers presented by a plant that is relatively carefree and nontemperamental. Therefore, I have lots of peonies but never purchased a single one; all were gifts from friends.

The lot upon which my house stands used to be double its size; but Mrs. Burton, the elderly widow from whom I purchased it, sold off the lot next door the year before I bought the house. The treasures that came with my house included two six-foot tall azalea bushes and a three-foot deep, eight-by-ten-foot, sixty-year-old compost pile behind the garage which is now my vegetable garden. The treasure that I coveted, however, was a long, healthy bed of herbaceous peonies planted on the far side of the lot Mrs. Burton sold.

It didn't take me long to meet the bachelor gentleman who had bought the lot and built his house on it. As luck would have it, he had no interest whatsoever in the peony bed; and when I asked for a division, he told me to take as many plants as I wanted. Nice man! I took several.

I have no idea of what variety these peonies are. They were planted so long ago that even my neighbor on the other side, Miss Dunham, who has lived in her house since her family bought it during World War II, says they were always there—not surprising news, actually, since peony beds are extremely long-lived.

I have other peonies too, all of which were gifts from friends. Two pink herbaceous peonies and a glorious magenta tree peony were brought from Michigan by a visiting friend. Another friend gave me my first white peony. Another was a gift from the mother of an old flame. The romance is history, but the plant is thriving!

Some of the peony gifts sulked for a year or so before blooming—the tree peony was the worst—but once they started they never stopped. They bloom in May and can be counted on to hold their blooms for up to six weeks, at which point they seem to sort of explode.

One day you have a plant in full bloom, and the next day you have a pile of petals. It happens indoors as well. Peonies make outstanding cut flowers and will maintain a fresh appearance for days and days; but when their time is up, they just suddenly shatter, and all you can do is get out the dust pan.

As I mentioned, once established, peonies are very self-reliant, and I have always found them to be trouble-free. Although they prefer a slightly acid pH, they flourish in a wide variety of soils as long as the bed drains quite freely. They do best in full sun but will thrive with partial shade in the late afternoon, especially in the warmer climates.

It's important to prepare a good site for the plants because they live a long time and deserve a rich soil mixture to grow in. Dig down at least a foot or more and mix in lots of compost, humus, well-rotted or composted manure, and a good helping of bone meal or superphosphate.

Peonies do best when planted or divided in autumn. One of the most important things to keep in mind when setting out peony plants is the depth at which they are planted. Each division should have a strong, fleshy root with at least three red buds on its surface. These buds, or eyes as they are often called, should be planted no more than one inch deep, and in warm climates as little as one-half inch deep. One of the main reasons peonies fail to bloom is that they have been planted too deeply. If you live in an extremely cold area, check with your local garden center for advice on planting depths.

Most peonies are exceedingly hardy, quite able to withstand temperatures well below zero, and they do somewhat better in cooler climates. They have few pests and diseases, so they require no spraying. They are heavy feeders, however, and benefit greatly from a feeding each spring of a fertilizer rich in bloom-boosting phosphates.

In spring, peony plants are covered with buds which mature at different times, and I find that I can lengthen the blooming period by immediately plucking any blossom which has begun to fade. Unlike many other perennials, once blooming has stopped peonies don't turn brown and keel over. Peony foliage will stay healthy and green right on through to the first frost, which makes an attractive backdrop for annuals and late-blooming perennials.

Staking is a necessary garden chore in growing peonies. Peony blooms are so large and

My peony blossoms were beautiful as cut flowers; but one day they quietly shattered, and I was left with a pile of lovely petals.

heavy, and their stems so slender and refined, that once in full bloom you are quite apt to find them lying prostrate in the garden unless you've had the foresight to provide some sort of support.

There are two easy ways to keep the plants upright. I keep a supply of bamboo stakes on hand and set three or four in the ground around each plant when it is almost ready to bloom.

The tree peony is a different kind of peony that is worth mentioning although not common. The name can cause disappointment in those who plant them expecting a tree to emerge laden with peony blooms. The plant does have woody stems but does not get much taller than its more popular herbaceous cousins. It is also a much slower growing plant, and all varieties are grafted. This combination of factors makes them very expensive. For many, however, the payoff is worth the cost and wait. The blooms are simply gigantic and unbelievably beautiful.

Another difference worth noting is that while herbaceous peonies hold their heads up and display their blooms proudly, the tree peony seems more shy, with the blooms often hidden among the delicately structured leaves. The blooms also grow quite close to the stem rather than on long stalks like those of the herbaceous varieties; and when cut for use indoors, they must be displayed in a shallow bowl or bud vase.

If you want to be remembered for a very long time by someone you hold dear, you could not do better than to bestow upon them a gift of peonies lifted from your own garden.

Deana Deck lives in Nashville, Tennessee, where her garden column is a regular feature in The Tennessean.

The Things I Prize

Garnett Ann Schultz

The fresh smell of the summer breeze,
The crimson of the skies,
The golden glint of morning's sun—
These are the things I prize—
The fragrance of a budding rose
With petals bright and wet.
The picture that I treasure most
Is God's own sweet sunset.

Just simple little untold joys
And love from someone dear—
I only want a heart content,
A mind that's free from fear.
I prize the wishes I can make,
The dreams that I can dream,
The pictures that my mind can paint,
So much I've never seen.

I wouldn't trade one precious note
Those little birds can sing;
I'll ever praise our God above
For every little thing.
The things I prize are oh so small,
So simple in their way—
A friendly smile because I'm loved
And needed every day.

I wouldn't want the greatest wealth;
I'd rather have a friend.
My heart can only know the peace
That love and kindness lend.
I have the world within my grasp
With pleasant sweet surprise,
And joys that life has given me—
These are the things I prize.

BITS & PIECES

A friendship true is like pure gold—
it won't wear out because it's old.
Harriett Meisenheimer

A friend is a word the very sight of which
in print makes the heart warm.
Augustine Birrell

A friend is a rare book, of which but one copy is made.
Author Unknown

We cannot tell the precise moment when friendship is formed. As in filling a vessel drop by drop, there is at last a drop which makes it run over; so in a series of kindnesses there is at last one which makes the heart run over.

Samuel Johnson

The only rose without thorns is friendship.
Madeleine de Scudéry

It is delightful to me to go mad
over a friend restored to me.
Horace

The most valuable antiques are old friends.
E. B. Birkenbeuel

PUHEK

Friendship is the great opportunity to demonstrate our capacity for lofty and ennobling relationships without the motive of selfishness.
Rosalie Mills Appleby

Friendship improves happiness and abates misery by doubling our joy and dividing our grief.
Joseph Addison

Friendship is the silver key that unlocks the door to happiness.
Ruth H. Underhill

My Friend

Vida I. Poutz

"This is my friend," I heard her say,
  And in her voice I heard
A certain something then relay
  That *friend* is no small word.

It seemed to pack a sort of pride;
  She wanted all to know
She had someone to stand beside,
  Someone in time of woe.

I heard her say, "This is my friend,"
  And that encompassed all—
Someone on whom you can depend
  To answer any call,

A certain sort of bond that held
  Through trouble and through strife,
Two common spirits closely bound
  In friendship all through life.

Deep inside a glow began
  And spread to warm my heart—
A feeling of deep gratitude
  For making me a part.

When she said, "This is my friend,"
  I knew she meant it too,
For in my heart she'd always held
  A space reserved for few.

Through the years true friends are made;
  You cannot beg or buy one.
But life has ways of sorting out,
  And time has tricks to try one.

As I look back, she always rose
  Far up above the rest,
And when she said, "This is my friend,"
  I knew I'd stood the test.

Understanding

Carice Williams

A pleasant smile is understood
By every race and creed,
And love finds joy in giving love
With every noble deed.

The language in a foreign land
May keep us far apart,
But loving smiles and kindly words
Unite us—heart to heart.

Be a friend to thyself, and
others will befriend thee.
—Proverb

FOR THE CHILDREN

ARTWORK BY RUSS FLINT

THE INVISIBLE PLAYMATE

Margaret Widdemer

When the other children go,
    Though there's no one seems to see
And there's no one seems to know,
    Fanny comes and plays with me.

She has yellow curly hair,
    And her dress is always blue.
And she always plays quite fair—
    Everything I tell her to.

People say she isn't there.
    They step over her at play,
And they sit down in her chair
    In the very rudest way.

It is queer they cannot know
    When she's there for me to see!
When the other children go,
    Fanny comes and plays with me.

The unique perspective of Russ Flint's artistic style has made him a favorite of Ideals *readers for many years. A resident of California and father of four, Russ Flint has illustrated a children's Bible and many other books.*

Kitty
(Eye to Eye)

JoAnn Stetka McPheron

Coaxing my pen with her cheek,
Ear nudging my hand,
She paws across my paper.

Flashing tail over my lashes,
Delivering her sandpaper kiss,
She sits on my idea.

Puppy Love

Carice Williams

A tiny, furry bundle,
Two eyes as black as night,
A warm pink tongue, like velvet,
Has charmed me with delight.
A tail that ne'er stops wagging
From morn till eventide,
My precious little puppy
Is now my joy and pride.

A Boy and His Dog

A boy and his dog make a glorious pair:
  No better friendship is found anywhere,
For they talk and they walk and they run and they play,
  And they have their deep secrets for many a day;
And that boy has a comrade who thinks and who feels,
  Who walks down the road with a dog at his heels.

He may go where he will, and his dog will be there;
  He may revel in mud, and his dog will not care;
Faithful he'll stay for the slightest command
  And bark with delight at the touch of his hand;
Oh, he owns a treasure which nobody steals,
  Who walks down the road with a dog at his heels.

No other can lure him away from his side;
  He's proof against riches and station and pride;
Fine dress does not charm him, and flattery's breath
  Is lost on the dog, for he's faithful to death;
He sees the great soul which the body conceals—
  Oh, it's great to be young with a dog at your heels!

Edgar A. Guest began his illustrious career in 1895 at the age of fourteen when his work first appeared in the Detroit Free Press. *His column was syndicated in over 300 newspapers, and he became known as "The Poet of the People."*

Do You Realize?

Craig E. Sathoff

I wonder if you realize
How much you mean to me
In bringing splendor to my day
When your glad smile I see.

And do you realize, my friend,
That when you send a letter,
You fill my day with warmth and cheer
Regardless of the weather?

Of course, you cannot realize
Those days before we met.
I was active, I was busy,
But I was rather lonely yet.

Your interests are so much like mine
That you bring new-found cheer
Into my mere existence now
Whenever you are near.

You've been a true and steadfast friend;
You've offered no disguise
To mask the values you possess,
And this I realize.

And I too like the older things,
The charm of bygone days,
The pleasures of companionship,
And simple homespun ways.

COUNTRY TREASURES
Jessie Walker Associates

Gillian and Susan playing jump-rope after school in September. USA 1944 →

Charles playing in front of his American home.

Photographs from FPG International. New York, New York.

British Youngsters Find Safe Havens in America

"Janie and I, we're a parade," seven-year-old Roddy explained. Carrying two small banners each—an American Stars and Stripes and a British Union Jack—the tow-headed pair had been hup-hupping down the quiet Long Island residential street.

"We got to have two flags," added Janie, who is six, "one for here, and one for home in England."

"It's because we have two countries," Roddy summed up. "We even have two presidents, Roosevelt and Churchill."

With unconscious eloquence the pair had expressed the deep, double loyalty of nearly 4,000 British youngsters who came here four years ago to escape the German bombing blitz. These wide-eyed, impressionable visitors have learned to love America and most things American. Yet their devotion to Britain is as wholehearted as ever. They are still attached to parents and friends, and even animal pets 3,000 miles across the sea.

As soon as their sections of England are safe

from enemy air attack—and shipping space is available—the young Britons will return. About twenty-five percent of the 1,000 evacuees brought here by the United States Committee for the Care of European Children have already sailed back. Rocket bombs may have held others here a little longer. But the daring experiment of transplanting thousands of youngsters to a strange environment far from home is now written into history as an extraordinary success.

It wasn't easy. Roddy and Janie, and even older children, landed here with vague and fantastic ideas of America.

"I'd heard about 'foster homes' and thought it meant an institution something like the one Oliver Twist was in," thirteen-year-old Ann confessed to a schoolmate. "Now I know there isn't anything as cruel as that in America."

Those first fears naturally proved groundless. Still American ways seemed strange.

"Everything was so different," Lisbeth, a long-legged redhead of eleven, recalls. "The way people talked and the funny words they used, the tall buildings, the new things we got to eat, and even the way people treated us. I didn't think I'd ever feel at home, as I do now."

American playmates bewildered the young guests. Their noisy play was "a bit rough," and their free and easy manners with adults seemed shocking.

Nevertheless, even the smallest tots turned up their thumbs and kept smiling. Adults were amazed at the absence of childish tears and tantrums.

For a long time, Jerrold, a fast-growing lad of seven, refused doggedly to exchange his English knickers for American clothes. At last he explained that his mother in parting had murmured, "I hope, Jerrold, you'll stay just as you are."

Jerrold meant to obey. He kept the outgrown knickers until his mother wrote for a photograph of him in American togs.

Nevertheless, it took a comparatively short time for American hosts and small British guests to understand and appreciate one another. The youngsters have now settled comfortably into their new ways of life. On the surface, they even appear to have been transformed into little Americans.

Roddy says "super" instead of "jolly"; he knows all about the Brooklyn Dodgers, but nothing about cricket teams; he is at home in skyscrapers and has the American small boy's fondness for ice-cream sodas and hot dogs. His English father is still "Daddy," but his American foster dad is greeted with "h'ya pop!"

Janie, who was only two when she arrived, demanded during a radio speech by Prime Minister Churchill, "Why does he talk so funny?" She was taken aback to learn that she too would talk that way after she had returned to England.

Tots and teenagers alike are planning to make many visits across the ocean. Some hope to attend American colleges. One nine-year-old has already announced his intention of returning to America "to marry." Above all, they are eager for parents and foster parents to meet after the war. One pair, waiting to sail for home, have chosen the dress they want their foster mother to wear when she follows later on.

An ocean doesn't seem a wide barrier to this young generation. As blond, blue-eyed Timmie says in his seven-year-old imagery:

"Boy, when an airplane goes zzzzzz-zoom, you zip a couple of miles in a minute. And there you are where you want to be!"

English parents who have been reunited with their offspring write approval of the changes four years have made. Of course, they are surprised at how tall and heavy their "babies" have grown. They find the repatriates well-mannered, though they manipulate knives and forks differently, and treat adults more casually than their young neighbors. Most striking of all is their self-reliance and mature sense of responsibility.

One of the older boys summed it up:

"All of us—from knee highs to big fellows—are a bit different now. We've had a big experience, and I'm sure it's going to make bigger men and women of us.

"We can't be just Britons any more." He hesitated, afraid he might sound too high-flown. "Maybe we can be those 'men of good will' I've heard about on the radio."

Originally printed in The Christian Science Monitor Magazine, *September 23, 1944.*

You Never Lose a Friend

Hilda Skott

You never lose a friend
E'en though your ways may part.
Each friend holds something dear
To keep within your heart.

We each must go our way
To live as we see fit;
Though parting may be sad,
We both can benefit.

The treasures from a friend
Live long in memory,
Yet years may pass before
Full worth of them we see.

As we share our lives,
Ourselves we get to know.
Much better we become;
In spirit and soul we grow.

We never lose a friend
E'en though our ways may part.
Each friend holds something dear
To keep within our hearts.

Friendship, Best of All

Louise Weibert Sutton

The world is my treasury; in it I find
The beauties of nature, of spirit, and mind—
Warm glories of sunrise, blue evening's first star,
And whippoorwills greeting the night from afar.
The rain is my silver, the sun is my gold,
And out in the garden are jewels untold:

Deep ruby-toned roses, soft emerald of fern,
The purple of pansies wherever I turn.
This world holds such blessings in ocean and sod,
With David I marvel the wonders of God:
Tall mountainous majesties, valleys that lie
Like gems in green velvet arched over the sky.

How wonderful merely to breathe the bright air,
To feel the blest kiss of the sun everywhere,
To walk in a springtime of hues without end,
Though the finest of all is the smile of a friend;
For heart speaks to heart, and the clasp of a hand
Is an eloquent language that all understand!

Earth's roses soon shatter, pink petals may fall,
The best castles crumble as time levels all.
Those jewels most prized may be stolen away,
And sunshine turn back to the winter's dull gray.
Yet friendship grows richer with age like rare wine,
And I am thrice-favored since yours has been mine!

Aunt Peggy

Sarah A. Heinzerling

I used to know the dearest lady,
A gray-haired lady, slim and tall;
Her bright eyes held the kindest twinkle
For neighbor children large or small.
She always smiled to see me coming,
The sort of smile that makes you glad;
I never saw her cross or angry,
And very seldom looking sad.

Oh my, the good things that she fed me!
Their recollection is sublime;
Each visit brought new, sweet surprises,
A different dainty every time—
One day, a slice of pound cake yellow,
The next, a wedge of custard pie,
Sometimes an apple, ripe and mellow,
Or candy kisses on the sly.

And oh, the flowers in her garden,
From which to cull a bright bouquet
Of blossoms to be loved a moment,
And in a moment cast away;
And yet she never once denied me
A flower that I longed to pull;
Instead, she often walked beside me
Until my greedy hands were full.

One day Aunt Peggy moved from our town,
The village where she played her part;
The memory of her kindness lingers
In my own grateful, loving heart.
I wish I too might leave behind me,
When I depart from kith and kin,
A garden of good deeds as fragrant
To blossom in the hearts of friends.

RAY HICKS, STORYTELLER, AT THE NATIONAL STORYTELLING FESTIVAL. Photograph by Tom Raymond, courtesy of the National Association for the Preservation and Perpetuation of Storytelling.

NATIONAL STORYTELLING FESTIVAL

Jonesborough, Tennessee

In every burg and hamlet across America, stories have been a mainstay of the people. Throughout the years, the people have told stories at barn raisings and quilting bees, cattle round-ups, and harvest feasts. They told the stories that have been passed down from generation to generation. Before the invention of the printing press, storytellers acted as the guardians of their people's history, preserving tales for future generations; and the storytellers who were the most talented in oral presentation were highly respected.

Today, the American people still treasure stories as deeply as did their ancestors. Ever since the bedtime rituals of early childhood, when we snuggled up to a parent to hear a favorite tale, we have loved storytelling. The advent of cinema, television, and videotape has taken its toll on this age-old medium; but in 1973, in a tiny Tennessee town in the heart of the southern Appalachian Mountains, the art of storytelling was reborn.

Jimmy Neil Smith, a school teacher living in Jonesborough, Tennessee, was driving along listening to his car radio when he heard one of his favorite tales told by storyteller Jerry Clower, a regular on the Grand Ole Opry. Clower spun a hilarious yarn about coon hunting in Mississippi that left Smith chuckling aloud and slapping his knee. It suddenly occurred to him how great it would be to bring storytellers all over America to Jonesborough to swap stories. Smith proposed the idea to the members of the Jonesborough Civic Trust, who responded positively. The Trust had been trying to develop a plan to restore historic Jonesborough and improve the town's economy. They jumped at Smith's idea, and he soon found himself organizing the first National Storytelling Festival.

Smith remembers that first festival fondly. He said, "On the second Saturday night in October of 1973, Jerry Clower—that same Mississippi coon hunter and storyteller—leapt to the stage in a hot, jammed high school gymnasium and told tales to over a thousand East Tennesseans. They had come for some side-splitting humor—the tales that had made Clower a household name throughout the Deep South. The crowd stomped and cheered, and they didn't leave disappointed.

"The following afternoon, we pulled an old farm wagon into Courthouse Square—in the shadow of the clock tower—and from that wagon, under a warm October sun, we told stories. They were there, the storytellers. A former Arkansas congressman. A Tennessee banker. A college professor. A western North Carolina farmer. They told their tales, and they breathed life into the first National Storytelling Festival."

The next year the festival attracted more and more listeners and storytellers, who met in parlors, front porches, and lawns throughout historic Jonesborough. Now with more than 6,000 guests and a wide array of storytelling talent, the National Storytelling Festival has blossomed into a grand event of international fame. Huge, colorful tents, food courts, and shuttle buses welcome visitors each October to this charming, 200-year-old town in the mountains of eastern Tennessee. Listeners and storytellers come to the mountains to celebrate America's rich and varied storytelling tradition. They come to hear old-fashioned folktales, updated fairy tales, the lore of Appalachia, Southern ghost

stories, the legends and myths of the Navaho people, cowboy poetry, and Brer Rabbit stories, to name but a few. The melting pot that is America is represented at the festival in its diverse list of featured tellers. Some tellers rely solely on their oral skill to entrance their audience, but others include mime acting, spoon playing, banjo picking, or even hoop spinning in their storytelling art. The Little Theatre of the Deaf, based in Chester, Connecticut, has performed some of the world's great tales to hearing and hearing-impaired audiences at the festival. Audience members can share the spotlight too at the Swappin' Ground, an area in the heart of the festivities where anyone can tell a story.

Festival celebrants can also choose from special programs for families and children, tellings of sacred tales, and additional concerts by renowned storytellers from around the globe. Area churches offer meals like "Old-Fashioned Cookin'" or "Pancake Breakfast," and a food tent, food court, and more concessions ensure that no one goes hungry.

The National Storytelling Festival is sponsored by the National Association for the Preservation and Perpetuation of Storytelling (NAPPS), a nonprofit organization founded in 1975 to help promote the practice, uses, and applications of the storytelling art. NAPPS is headquartered in Jonesborough, Tennessee, and led by none other than Jimmy Neil Smith, executive director and founder of the National Storytelling Festival.

Storytelling has always been an important part of our unique heritage as Americans, and the people of America cherish their stories. The "rebirth" of storytelling in America has encouraged many people to discover and begin to tell the stories in their lives. Some tellers have realized their true talents lie in spinning tales for listeners, in communicating emotions, adventure, and humor on an intimate basis with an audience. Tellers make a connection with their audience that is simply not possible in the electronic mediums; the intimacy is lost. Celebrants at the National Storytelling Festival experience that connection with the tellers again and again. They leave with new stories to pass on to their friends and families, and in doing so they keep the art of storytelling alive.

Nancy Skarmeas

Joel Chandler Harris
Writer

Joel Chandler Harris, born in 1848, grew up in poverty in rural Georgia. The son of an Irish-born day laborer, Harris was a shy young boy with a keen sense of humor and a highly developed habit of quiet but astute observation. In his early teen years, he had the good fortune to be accepted as an apprentice to Joseph Addison Turner, the owner of a nearby plantation in Eatonton, Georgia, and publisher of a literary newspaper called *The Countryman.* Harris began his training as a typesetter, but he also took advantage of Turner's vast library and his generous tutoring in English grammar and literature.

It was on Turner's plantation that Harris heard the slaves repeat the humorous animal stories and African lore that later became the creative impetus for his Uncle Remus stories. Harris was captivated by the rich, cohesive culture of the African-American families; and as an adult, he recalled his youth in pre-Civil War Georgia and those memorable tales that had enchanted him. The result was the "Uncle Remus" stories. By the late nineteenth century, this collection of folktales won Harris comparisons with the great American storyteller Mark Twain.

Although his family was poor, Harris lived a comfortable life as part of the great apparatus of a successful plantation. He grew to adulthood, therefore, with little knowledge of the world outside the South. By 1866, when Turner's plantation went bankrupt after the devastation of the Civil War, Harris had sufficient training and education to get a job as a typesetter in Macon. He later landed a position at the Savannah *Morning News,* where he had his first regular column called "Affairs in Georgia"—a combination of humorous sketches and observations on local life. It was in Savannah that Harris first began to gain the attention of the public for his humorous portrayal of the Southern culture of that time.

In 1876 Harris accepted a position at the Atlanta *Constitution,* one of the largest newspapers in the South, and stayed with the paper for the next twenty-four years. It was in the pages of the *Constitution* that his first Uncle Remus stories appeared. These were the animal fables featuring Brer Rabbit—who relies on his wit to survive a series of mishaps and difficult situations— that were based on the African folklore

Harris had heard the slaves recount on the Eatonton plantation. Writing in the African-American dialect he had absorbed in this setting, Harris presented these tales via the fictional Uncle Remus, who recounts them to an attentive and adoring young boy. Harris experienced immediate and overwhelming success. The Uncle Remus stories were praised for their authentic dialect and embraced not only by readers across the nation but also across the globe; eventually, the Uncle Remus stories were translated into every living language. Several Uncle Remus books followed, as did other stories of life in rural Georgia before the war. In all, Harris authored twenty books during his lifetime of writing. His work inspired a whole group of Southern writers intent on documenting the unique way of life of plantation days. Almost forty years after his death in 1908, Harris's Uncle Remus stories were immortalized forever in the Walt Disney classic movie *Song of the South,* which told the stories to another generation of children and guaranteed that Uncle Remus would be a lasting part of American culture.

Joel Chandler Harris was one of the first great American storytellers, a true pioneer in this literary art form. He renewed the tradition of telling animal stories—a tradition that dates back to Aesop—in millions of homes around the world. His Uncle Remus stories endure as a part of American cultural history and preserve the sound of an early African-American dialect that might otherwise have been lost to the passage of time. The tales are a virtual treasure trove for students and collectors of American folklore, who have discovered the original charm of the stories that inspired Harris years ago. For all with a love of history and an appreciation of good storytelling, the work of Joel Chandler Harris provides an artfully written, personal depiction of a unique time and place in American history.

Friendly Neighbors

Harriet Whipple

It's a joy to have a neighbor
Who offers friendship too—
A blessing to be cherished
That means so much to you—

One who shares a joy or sorrow,
Who always understands,
One that you can count upon
To lend a helping hand.

It is like a flower garden
One fills with little seeds
That we need to cultivate
With love and thoughtful deeds.

If you want a friendly neighbor,
Be sure to be one too;
Friendship's like a boomerang
That comes right back to you.

OLD TREASURES

Jennie Moulton

We love the gleam and sparkle
Of old china rich and rare,
The brilliance of old tarnished gems
Restored with patient care;
We prize old treasured keepsakes
With dust of time o'er cast,
Old valentines and letters,
Cherished memories of the past.

We love old wrinkled faces
With all the marks they bear
Of sunny smiles and laughter
That long have lingered there;
We trace the hope and courage,
The love beyond compare
That shines anew from faces
Adorned with silver hair.

But by far the richest treasures,
And those we love the best,
Are the dear old friends so faithful
Whose love has stood the test;
They have shared our joys and sorrows
Always with an outstretched hand,
Giving help and strength and comfort
From true hearts that understand.

A Prayer

Martha Epperson

God grant that I may always see
Beauty just next door to me
    In a friendly smile
    Or a happy child
Or china cups filled up with tea,

Or maybe in a cheerful day
Or kittens on the lawn at play,
    Some leaves to rake,
    A hand to shake,
The altar where I kneel to pray;

And beauty in a word that cheers
In friendship lasting through the years,
    A harsh word spared,
    And sorrows shared,
Rainbows there to catch the tears.

So long as I can find these here,
These lovely things that I hold dear,
    Your lovely ways,
    Our happy days,
I know I'll never learn to fear.

CHURCH IN THE VILLAGE OF ST. HUBERTS
Adirondack Mountains, New York
Jeff Gnass Photography

BOOK COLLECTING

Lisa C. Thompson

Almost all of us are book collectors in a way. We acquire books, and for one reason or another, we keep them. The true collector, however, has a method to the madness. Bibliophiles, as these lovers of books are called, are highly organized, zealous buyers who harbor a small fire burning deep within them that blazes a little brighter and a little hotter with each new purchase.

Books are an ideal investment for many reasons, including the opportunity to enjoy your investment daily—by reading! Money invested in a book collection is almost invariably well spent, especially if you are lucky enough to purchase a rare out-of-print edition since rare books usually appreciate every year.

The idea that book collecting is best suited for an elite few who have the leisure and funds to seek out and purchase expensive rare books is a misguided conception. Book collecting is for anyone who loves books; and a lot of money, education, or spare time is not a requirement. Some collectors begin by acquiring books on a specific subject or by a certain author. You may already have a connected theme resting on your bookshelves. Take a few moments to rediscover your books and note any similarities. Your interests will lead you naturally to the area in which you will want to expand your collection.

To the collector, the term first edition refers to the copies of a book that come from the first printing. If the publisher discovers an error in the first printing, a second printing might be ordered with the correction in place. This second printing is then a second issue. To the publisher, it is the second issue of the first edition, but the *true* first edition to the bibliophile is the book that contains the error. The first issue of the first edition is the most desirable and will fetch the highest price. First editions of out-of-print books are hard to come by and usually expensive, but not all are rare. Rarity comes with desirability. An unpopular book may have special meaning to a certain collector, but that does not make the first edition of that book worth thousands.

THE LIBRARY WALL
H. Armstrong Roberts

We all dream of that moment when browsing through a dusty second-hand bookshop we uncover a first edition of Dickens' *A Christmas Carol,* but reality belies the fantasy. Acquiring a first edition is a tedious, painstaking process to be accomplished by only the most dedicated, diligent collector and involves an array of specialized dealers and librarians. A simpler way to acquire a first edition book is to consider first editions from major living authors that fit your collection. Scurry to the bookstore as soon as the book is for sale and beware of the stamp of doom "second impression before publication," which can happen if a publisher orders another press run before the first copies are in the stores.

Other desirable types of books are association copies, signed copies, or presentation copies. Association copies have indications such as an autograph, inscription, marginal notes, or bookplate that connects the book with the author or someone close to the author. A signed copy includes the signature of the author or illustrator. A presentation copy is a book inscribed by the author and presented as a gift to a family member, literary person, or other famous figure. Some bibliophiles covet presentation copies as much as first editions.

A library or a bookstore can be a great starting place in which to learn more about adding books to your collection. A reference librarian can lead you to source books, trade directories, and periodicals to aid you in your research. Slowly you can begin to develop a bibliography of books in your subject area.

Books can be bought and sold in several different ways, but bear in mind that book collecting does not offer a rapid return on your investment. Selling books can be a slow process because it may take some time to find a buyer. Book auctions, estate auctions, book fairs, antiquarian bookshops, private dealers, and other collectors all are sources for book trading. Sometimes public libraries and universities sell books as well. Every collector should become acquainted with several book dealers. Some second-hand dealers work via mail services and may take appointments for private viewings. Certain dealers at second-hand or antiquarian bookshops will search for out-of-print books for you. Experienced collectors suggest that in working with several dealers, you do not send mass mailings of your wants list.

This can result in an artificially high price when several dealers advertise for the same book, thereby falsely implying a great demand.

When assembling your book collection and arranging it to your taste, create a catalog listing of the title and author of every book in your library. Many bibliophiles maintain meticulous catalog entries which list all known information about the books in their collection. Your catalog will be helpful when comparing it to the bibliography of your selected subject and also to provide valuable proof to the insurance company in case of fire or theft.

Proper care of any book collection is essential. Experts agree that books should be stored in bookcases with glass doors out of direct sunlight in a cool room with an ideal relative humidity of around fifty percent. The books should not be packed too tightly on the shelves, and if metal bookends are used, cardboard should be placed between each bookend and the book it supports to prevent scarring or tearing of the book's cover. If you do discover a flaw of this kind, do not attempt home repairs but rather locate a book repair expert. Many kinds of tape and glues contain chemicals that are damaging to books, and a do-it-yourselfer often ends up with a book in worse condition than before. Rubber bands, paper clips, staples, epoxy, ball-point pens, and felt-tip pens are also highly detrimental to the life of your books. Bookplates, a bibliophile's personal labels, should be affixed with plain library starch paste.

Incandescent lighting is less destructive to paper than fluorescent lighting and therefore better for your collection. In addition to proper lighting, library hygiene must be maintained. Your books and shelves should be dusted regularly and inspected for pests such as the bookworm or the booklouse, which do not discriminate between new and old books; they will devour your rare copy of Kafka's *The Metamorphosis* and your current telephone directory with equal enthusiasm.

With all the research, buying, selling, arranging, cataloging, and cleaning that is part of book collecting, one final admonition must be heard: Don't get so wrapped up in the process of collecting that you forget to *enjoy* your collection. Read your books and relish their meaning in your life. Isn't that why you started collecting books in the first place?

Handmade Heirloom

Mary Skarmeas

CROSS-STITCHED BOOKMARKS. All models designed and stitched for DMC by Judith M. Chrispens except the "L" and "Friend" bookmarks, which were stitched by the author. Photography by Gerald Koser.

BOOKMARKS

With the easy availability—and disposability—of paper bookmarks at libraries and bookstores, we do not readily think of bookmarks as heirlooms; and in our rush to finish quilts for the grandchildren's cribs and hand-knit sweaters for the family at Christmastime, we likely never consider the tiny bookmark as an outlet for our creative skills. But bookmarks have a history as old as books themselves, and for most of that history, they were skillfully and lovingly hand-crafted to commemorate a special occasion or to express love or friendship. The bookmark deserves a second look; it is a craft that requires neither a great commitment of time nor a considerable outlay of money, but one that

will certainly find a lasting place in every home.

The first bookmarks were simple, narrow ribbons bound into the spines of Bibles and prayer books. For ministers, these ribbons marked the chosen passages for Sunday sermons; at home, ribbons kept the place of favorite psalms or cherished verses. Anchored ribbon bookmarks can still be found in Bibles and fine hardcover volumes today. But the bookmark was not destined to be forever bound to the book. Like many other "practical" crafts, the bookmark began as a purely utilitarian item; but with imagination, creative flair, and the irresistible human need to add beauty to life, it evolved into a delightful handicraft.

The first detached bookmarks date back almost as far as the original anchored variety, but it was in the nineteenth century that women in England and America truly discovered the art of the bookmark. Upper- and middle-class women with leisure time and embroidery skills found stitching detailed designs on ribbon a rewarding way to pass the hours. In families with more practical concerns, the small size of the bookmark proved ideal for young girls practicing their needlework. And in every home a handmade bookmark was a lovely complement to the family Bible, prayer book, or any treasured volume.

Bookmarks were made with whatever was on hand: paper, silk, ribbon, fabric scraps, leather. They were decorated with cross-stitching, needlepoint, embroidery, dyes, and even watercolors. Bookmark designs incorporated religious symbols, proverbs, psalms, names, and holiday themes as well as the dates of births, weddings, christenings, and other family milestones, much as they still do today. The height of the bookmark craze was in the 1860s, when silk bookmarks made by Thomas Stevens of Coventry, England, became popular. Stevengraphs, as they were known, were little pictures woven onto silk fabric which was then cut into rectangular strips and decorated with fringe and a tassel. Stevengraphs featured poems, psalms, holiday themes, celebrity portraits, and country scenes; they immediately became a coveted collectible. The availability of Stevengraphs and their many imitators did nothing to slow the hands of the many crafters producing their own handmade bookmarks. If anything, the Stevengraph craze simply gave them new inspiration.

Perhaps the most popular handmade bookmark from the middle to late nineteenth century—one made by women and girls all across America—was the charming cross-stitched marker which resembled a miniature sampler. Cross-stitched bookmarks were worked on pre-stamped paper or on plain fabric. The designs were as numerous as the stitchers, and each bookmark was an expression of the creator's personality and a display of their needlework skills. A typical American cross-stitched bookmark featured a simple message such as "love" or "friend," a short Bible verse, or a favorite motto stitched down the length of the bookmark with a border of decorative stitching. For young stitchers lacking the coordination and the attention span for larger, more complex projects, the cross-stitched bookmark was the perfect beginner's project; for the more skilled needleworkers, bookmarks provided a break from large projects and an outlet for creative experimentation. After stitching was complete, the bookmarks were decorated with wide strips of colorful ribbon for backing and were often given as gifts to family and friends to commemorate special occasions.

The heirloom quality of handmade bookmarks is verified by their growing popularity as a collectible. Neither expensive nor fragile, bookmarks appeal to the collector looking for something that provides a personal connection to a time gone by, evidence of a common thread between past generations and our own. There are clubs, conventions, and even a newsletter for bookmark collectors.

Just as antique bookmarks connect us to the past, those made by our own hands today can link us to the future by serving its useful purpose for many years to come. A classic American cross-stitched bookmark can be easily recreated. Those familiar with counted cross-stitch may choose to create their own designs on scraps of fabric left over from larger projects; a border stitched either by machine or hand will keep a frayed edge from unraveling. Perforated paper and vinyl weave are other options available in a wide variety of colors, and inexpensive cotton embroidery floss comes in any color imaginable. The skills of cross-stitching are easy to learn. Beginner books abound with pre-printed designs to guide every stitch; or with graph paper and a pencil, you can create your own. With practice, the cross-stitched bookmark becomes a canvas limited only by the imagination of the crafter.

The bookmark—a most useful and practical item—provides a wonderful craft for the stitcher looking for a project that is quick to make but results in a keepsake that can last through the years. And once you have replaced every bookstore or library bookmark with one made by your own hands, you will agree that even the most beloved book becomes a little more special when its pages are graced by a beautiful, handcrafted bookmark.

Mary Skarmeas lives in Danvers, Massachusetts, and is studying for her bachelor's degree in English at Suffolk University. Mother of four and grandmother of one, Mary loves all crafts, especially knitting.

"Letters mingle souls."

–John Donne

Miss Charlotte Brontë
Haworth, England

Miss Ellen Nussey
London
England

My Dear Liszt:
I must say, <u>you are a friend</u>. Let me say no more to you, for although I always recognized in friendship between men the noblest and highest relation, it was you who embodied this idea into its fullest reality by letting me no longer imagine, but feel and grasp, what a friend is. I do not thank you, for you alone have the power to thank yourself by your joy in being what you are. It is noble to have a friend, but still nobler to be a friend.
Richard Wagner

Haworth
June 19th, 1834

My own dear Ellen [Nussey],
I may rightfully and truly call you so <u>now</u>. You <u>have</u> returned, or are returning from London, from the great city which to me is almost apocryphal as Babylon or Nineveh, or ancient Rome. You are withdrawing from the world (as it is called) and bringing with you, if your letters enable me to form a correct judgment, a heart as unsophisticated, as natural, as true, as that you carried there. . . . How many after having, as they thought, discovered the word friend in the mental volume, have afterwards found they should have read <u>false</u> friend! I have long seen "friend" in your mind, in your words, in your actions, but <u>now</u> distinctly visible, and clearly written in characters that cannot be distrusted, I discern <u>true</u> friend! I am really grateful for your mindfulness of so obscure a person as myself, and I hope the pleasure is not altogether selfish; I trust it is partly derived from the consciousness that my friend's character is of a higher, a more steadfast order than I was once perfectly aware of. Few girls would have done as you have done—would have beheld the glare and glitter and dazzling display of London, with the disposition so unchanged, hearts so uncontaminated. I see no affectation in your letter, no trifling, no frivolous contempt of plain, and weak admiration of showy persons and things.

Charlotte Brontë

Torquay
Friday, November 13, 1838

You dearest Miss [Mary Russell] Mitford,
Whenever I forget to notice any kindness of yours, do
believe, my beloved friend, that I have, notwithstanding,
marked the date of it with a white stone, and also with a
heart _not_ of stone. . . .

    Dearest, dearest, Miss Mitford, never, _never_ do tear up
any old letters of yours for the sake of sending me a new
one. Send old and new together. Postage upon _your_ letters
never can be thought of, and besides, my correspondents are
not like yours, millions in the way of numbers. They in
Wimpole Street know my doxy upon such subjects too well
to keep your letters back with the seeds. They did not _dare_
to wait even a day for papa's coming, but sent it out at once
to me, doubtless it was, and _in_ a letter of Arabel's own,
making a triple; and those "discerning spirits" at the post
office marked it (for all the thick paper) a _single letter_ —
immortal essence not weighing anything. . . .

    Elizabeth Barrett Browning

Passy
January 27, 1783
Dear Mrs. Hewson,
In looking forward, twenty-five years seems a long period; but, in looking back, how short! Could you imagine
that it is now full a quarter of a century since we were
first acquainted? It was in 1757. During the greatest part
of this time I lived in the same house with my dear
deceased friend, your mother; of course you and I saw and
conversed with each other much and often. It is all to our
honor, that, in all that time, we never had among us the
smallest misunderstanding. Our friendship has been all
clear sunshine, without any, the least, clouds in its hemi-
sphere. Let me conclude by saying to you what I have had
too frequent occasion to say to my other remaining old
friends: the fewer we become, the more let us love one
another.
Adieu, etc.
Benjamin Franklin

THROUGH MY WINDOW

Pamela Kennedy

Art by Russ Flint

JUST A NOTE

As I pull into the garage, I feel a bump and hear the crunch of plastic and metal. After extricating myself and two bags of groceries from the car, I peer under the wheels. Robo the Robot has suffered decapitation. There is something plaintive in the plastic button eyes as they gaze up into mine. That is how my son will look when I tell him Robo is dead. I am angry that I will have to bring the disappointment, angry that he has been so careless.

Sighing, I hitch up the groceries and dash through the downpour to the back door, taking a direct route through the only puddle in the driveway. Soaked and frustrated, I fumble for the key, unlock the door, and stumble into the laundry room, almost tripping over abandoned hats and coats. "Who left all this stuff lying around!?" I shout, but only the bored hum of the refrigerator answers me.

After dumping the dripping groceries on the counter, I slosh to the front hall to retrieve the day's offerings from the mail slot:

"Catalogue of Unbelievable Values!!!"
"Important, Do Not Discard!"
"You Are One of a Select Few . . ."
"Occupant"
"Informed Citizen"
A small, unpretentious blue envelope is tucked under the stack of junk mail. The return address is that of a friend. I open it and find a card with a border of forget-me-nots surrounding the words "Just a Note . . ." Inside it reads:

I've been meaning to drop a line for so long just to let you know how much I appreciate your smile and words of encouragement. Thanks for being you.

I read the last sentence again and cannot stifle an ironic smile—wet, angry, bedraggled, yet appreciated. I feel the tingle of tears welling. Just a note? Hardly.

It turns my day around. I stow my damp groceries, dry my shoes, and retrieve Robo's remains. By three thirty, when my son comes home from school, Robo has almost fully recovered from major plastic surgery.

"He'll be fine." I assure my dubious child. "One more laser treatment and he'll be good as new. Have a cookie." I smile. Just a note.

I hum an old love song as I fix supper. Then, for no real reason, I cut up radishes to look like roses and decorate the meatloaf slices with red blossoms and green parsley leaves.

"What's this?" my husband asks, frowning at his bedecked meatloaf.

"Elegance," I reply.

"If you say so, dear." He crunches into a radish rose, lifting his little finger delicately.

I laugh at his dramatics and shake my head slightly. Just a note.

That night, as the kids sleep and my husband reads the newspaper, I re-read the forget-me-not note. My thoughts wander back in time to other words of encouragement, written by loving hands and hearts and received, somehow, at just the right time.

I recall a note scribbled on a paper napkin and tucked into a lunch bag by a mother who sensed the insecurity heralded by cheerleader tryouts. There was a note slipped into an algebra book by a friend who knew the hurt of breaking up. I remember a note left with a plant, welcoming us to our first apartment, and another sent to encourage us when we had to move across the country.

Just a note? When someone takes the time to put pen to paper, when another person commits herself in writing, something beautiful takes place. A fragment of the soul is shared, a bit of the heart revealed.

I glance at the rain still falling in the darkness and watch the drops smearing down the windows in the streetlight's glare—one alone, then two together, pushing into three, then countless drops cascading to the sill. That's how it is, I think. One reaches out a little to another, then another. The caring gains momentum. It doesn't have to stop.

Compelled by the raindrops' revelation, I search in the old roll-top desk. In the bottom drawer, under the clutter of gift wrap, tissue, and Christmas tags, I find a box of note cards. Pouring a cup of tea, I sit at the kitchen table and make a list: the crossing guard who is always at the corner, rain or shine, the teacher who struggled through the report on dinosaurs with my daughter, my mother, who perhaps never knew how much her encouragement meant. I wouldn't compose a lengthy letter. No, I'd write . . . just a note.

Pamela Kennedy is a free-lance writer of short stories, articles, essays, and children's books. Wife of a naval officer and mother of three children, she has made her home on both U.S. coasts and currently resides in Honolulu, Hawaii. She draws her material from her own experiences and memories, adding bits of her imagination to create a story or mood.

Good Talk

Henry Van Dyke

The very best thing is good talk, and the thing that helps it most is *friendship.* How it dissolves the barriers that divide us, and loosens all constraints, and diffuses itself like some fine old cordial through all the veins of life—this feeling that we understand and trust each other, and wish each other heartily well! Everything into which it really comes is good. It transforms letter-writing from a task to a pleasure. It makes music a thousand times more sweet. The people who play and sing not *at us,* but *to us,*—how delightful it is to listen to them! Yes, there is a talkability that can express itself even without words. There is an exchange of thoughts and feeling which is happily alike in speech and in silence. It is quietness pervaded with friendship.

Something about a Coffee Cup

Marje LaBrache

There's something about a coffee cup
　　That sets a neighbor down,
That lifts her sagging spirits up
　　And steams away her frown.

There's something about the beany brew
　　That warms a caller's smile,
That lets her know her visit's due
　　And bids her stay awhile.

There's something about a perking pot
　　That sweetens up the air
And promises a cup of hot
　　With time to linger there.

There's something about a coffee cup
　　That sets an atmosphere
Of hearts and handles lifted up
　　And says, "I'm glad you're here."

Ideals'
Family Recipes

Favorite Recipes from the Ideals Family of Readers

Editor's Note: If you would like us to consider your favorite recipe, please send a typed copy of the recipe along with your name, address, and phone number to *Ideals* Magazine, ATTN: Recipes, P.O. Box 148000, Nashville, Tennessee 37214-8000. We will pay $10 for each recipe used. Recipes cannot be returned.

VINTAGE FRUIT SAUCE

Here's a recipe for fermented fruit from our friends at Red Star Yeast and Products, a division of Universal Foods. The starter makes enough for two batches of sauce, so you can share a starter with a friend.

Vintage Fruit—In a glass jar with a loose cover, such as an apothecary's jar, combine ¾ cup canned peaches in heavy syrup, drained and cut into pieces, ¾ cup canned pineapple tidbits in heavy syrup, drained, six maraschino cherries, halved, 1½ cups granulated sugar, and one package of instant dry yeast. Stir several times the first day, then stir once a day for two weeks. Do not store in refrigerator during the fermenting process.

Vintage Fruit Sauce—Remove one cup of Vintage Fruit from glass jar and place in decorative glass jar for a friend. To remaining fruit, add ½ cup canned peaches in heavy syrup, drained and cut into pieces, ½ cup canned pineapple tidbits in heavy syrup, drained, six maraschino cherries, halved, and one cup granulated sugar. Stir well. Set in fairly warm place. Stir once a day for one week; the sauce is ready to be served after one week. Fruit and sugar must be added every two weeks if you want to keep your vintage fruit sauce.

Vintage Salad Ring

In a large mixing bowl, add 2 cups boiling water to two 3-ounce packages lemon flavored gelatin; stir to dissolve. Add ½ cup cold water.

Transfer 1 cup of gelatin mixture to a separate mixing bowl; add ½ cup Vintage Fruit Sauce to first mixing bowl; pour into greased 6-cup ring mold; chill until clear.

To remaining cup of gelatin, add 1 cup sour cream; mix thoroughly, and chill until thickened. Add 1 cup Vintage Fruit Sauce to creamy mixture. Pour over layer in mold and chill until firm.

Vintage Sweet Potato Bake

Drain and slice thickly one 30-ounce can sweet potatoes. Place sweet potatoes in 1-quart casserole. Spoon ¾ cup drained Vintage Fruit over potatoes.

In a small saucepan, combine ½ cup Vintage Fruit syrup, 2 tablespoons packed brown sugar, ¼ teaspoon salt, and 2 tablespoons butter or margarine; cook over medium heat until butter has melted. Pour over sweet potatoes.

Bake in a preheated 350° oven for 15 minutes; sprinkle with ¼ cup flaked coconut and continue to bake until coconut is browned, about 15 minutes.

Heavenly Vintage Dessert

Prepare one 5.1-ounce package vanilla pudding according to package directions. Slice one loaf of prepared angel food cake into ½-inch slices. Arrange half of the slices to cover bottom of ungreased 9-x-13-inch pan.

In a medium mixing bowl, combine pudding and 1 cup drained Vintage Fruit; fold in 1 cup whipped cream or whipped topping. Spoon half of pudding mixture evenly over cake slices in pan; cover with remaining cake slices and top with remaining pudding mixture.

Cover and refrigerate at least 4 hours. Garnish with toasted slivered almonds, if desired.

Autumn Potpourri

Nora M. Bozeman

Maple trees of crimson,
Oaks and sumacs red,
Orange pumpkins in a row,
Cloud wisps overhead,

Mums in multicolors,
Full moon on the rise,
Wild geese winging southward,
Golds that hypnotize—

Scarlet days of autumn
On the ground have shed.
Snowflakes soon will tumble
When fall and winter wed.

Readers' Reflections

Editor's Note: Readers are invited to submit unpublished, original poetry for possible publication in future issues of Ideals. Please send copies only; manuscripts will not be returned. Writers receive $10 for each published submission. Send material to "Readers' Reflections," Ideals Publications Inc., P.O. Box 148000, Nashville, TN 37214-8000.

Friends

Friends are like jewels that sparkle and shine:
You cherish them more with the passing of time.

Friends are like trees that bend with the wind:
They give you the strength to stand straight once again.

Friends are like flowers that add beauty to life:
They help see you through your heartaches and strife.

God must have known in his infinite way
To give you a friend would help make your day.

Helene Notestine
LaGrange, Indiana

Hello, New Friend

Hello, my new friend,
I'm so glad you've come my way.
In the short life of our friendship,
There's so much I want to say.

To start with let me thank you
For seeing something there in me
That drew you to this world of mine
For whatever that may be.

I feel we're kindred spirits
In a space all of our own.
Just to know you feel the way I do
Makes me feel not so alone.

How nice to talk and share with you,
Not have to watch my p's and q's.
You make me laugh, you're good for me,
And I hope I'm good for you.

Linda Emmons
Grand Prairie, Texas

Old Friends in the Attic

I've got old friends in the attic
 Of curiosity—
Collections of the things I love
 And care for tenderly.
I climb the creaky staircase
 Into nostalgic bliss,
And in this loft, in heartfelt thought,
 I sit and reminisce.

My old gingham dog stands steadfast;
 We shared bold escapades
With my horse who rocked our course
 Through childhood masquerades.
And that patch quilt brought me comfort
 On nights Mom read to me,
But though it's old and threadbare cold,
 It warms my memory.

There's the Philco from the parlor;
 It gave us all a thrill.
Ah, those shows on radio—
 My memory hears them still.
And on rafters near the window
 Hang ribbons, mostly blue,
'Cause at the fair, none could compare
 With pumpkins that I grew.

In boxes, bags, and bureau drawers,
 Old friends are waiting there—
Dingy stuff that I dust off
 With gentleness and care.
And in those quiet moments of
 Reflections on the past,
I've come to know things come and go
 But friendships last and last.

Lon Myruski
Washingtonville, New York

Taking Time

You'll find that life is richer
 If you take the time to do
The very things that you would want
 Your friends to do for you.

Take time to keep a promise
 Or send a card of cheer.
Call an old forgotten friend
 To say that you're still here.

Take time to mend a quarrel,
 Express a gratitude,
Invite a friend to dinner,
 Show a helping attitude.

Take time to share a child's dream;
 Be patient for a day;
Learn to count from one to ten
 When children disobey.

You'll be surprised how good you feel,
 The happiness it brings,
If you take time to do for others
 Loving, thoughtful things.

So grab onto the golden rule;
 Do unto others too,
And very soon you'll notice
 Your friends take time for you.

Ellen Zapf
Adams Center, New York

October

Helen Jackson

Bending above the spicy woods which blaze,
Arch skies so blue they flash and hold the sun
Immeasurably far; the waters run
Too slow, so freighted are the riverways
With gold of elms and birches from the maze
Of forests. Chestnuts, clicking one by one,
Escape from satin burs; her fringes done,
The gentian spreads them out in sunny days;
And like late revellers at dawn, the chance
Of one sweet, mad, last hour all things assail
And, conquering, flush and spin while, to enhance
The spell by sunset door, wrapped in a veil
Of red and purple mists, the summer, pale,
Steals back along for one more song and dance.

Song for October

William Arnette Wofford

The leaves are blowing on the wind
   And fall beside the garden wall;
But still defeating early frost,
   Chrysanthemums stand proudly tall.

Fox grapes hang purple in the wood
   Where summer's wild azaleas glowed;

And apples have turned darkest red
 Upon the hawthorn by the road.

The dogwoods are a scarlet flame;
 The pears hang golden overhead;
Ripe chestnuts fall upon the path
 Where crimson woodbine runners spread.

The reapers in the dell are heard;
 And wagons move across the field,
Carrying the grain up to the barn
 That now awaits the harvest yield.

Cling to October's golden days
 Before they fade and soon depart;
Treasure this glory of the year
 And store it safe within your heart!

Autumnal Equinox

Ruth Marie Katchentz

Through summer's wealth
of golden days
There comes a time
for season's ending,
And there appears
with autumn's blaze
A certain look
of winter pending.

As shadows lengthen
on the lawn,
The gardens pale
and cease their blooming,
And days will shrink
from dusk to dawn
From barren sight
of winter looming.

When night and day
their hours swing
And summer fades
with autumn's crossing,
The changing equinox
will bring
A breath of spring
in winter's tossing.

Gay October

Beverly J. Anderson

I love this season of the year
When days are crisp and honey-clear,
When painted leaves come tumbling down
In hues of crimson, ocher, brown.

I love to seek a country way
When autumn time is in full sway,
When scarlet sumacs wave and nod
To asters and to goldenrod,

When hillsides far as eye can see
Look like a patchwork tapestry,
When autumn's sky is brilliant blue
And sunbeams glimmer all in view.

I love to walk 'mid beauty rare
When autumn joy is everywhere,
When nature has a peace to lend
As gay October's colors blend.

ASPEN
City of Rocks National Reserve
Albion Mountains, Idaho
Jeff Gnass Photography

Renewal

Paul Swope

Autumn's here, and all around us
    Earth smiles with a russet face
While the paintbrush of the season
    Wipes out summer's last green trace.

Robins fluff their feathers outward,
    Fending off the chill of night;

At the first gold ray of morning
  They'll begin their southern flight.

Soon cold fingers pull the cover
  Of snow blankets to Earth's chin,
And the small beasts of the woodland
  Brace for winter to begin.

But, though icy winds are howling
  While bare branches wildly swing,
Deep beneath the frozen mantle
  Grow green promises of spring!

Readers' Forum

Meet Our Ideals Readers and Their Families

DICK HOUGHTON of Lancaster, Pennsylvania, creates collages in his spare time with the pictures from *Ideals* and other magazines. He even sent us the collage on the right because he filled it with pictures from copies of *Ideals* he had saved through the years. Dick has been pursuing his hobby since he retired in 1980 and estimates that over 3,000 collages created from his hands are "out there" among friends and family members. Dick made friends with some truck drivers, and soon his "Hand Crafted Time Creations," as he calls them, were all over the country. The collages are usually centered around a specific theme and often include a clock, hence the name.

Dick has been subscribing to *Ideals* for more years than he can remember and has always thought the beautiful pictures were too pretty to throw away.

Thank you, Dick, for sharing your hobby with us!

MARGARET WEIDEMAN of Walton, Kentucky, sent us this photograph of her granddaughter, Molly Michelle, who is already a clotheshorse at age six. Molly lives in Harrison, Ohio, with her parents, Steve and Laurie Weideman, and her two sisters, Bethany Joy and Carrie Marie. Molly loves to go to Sunday school and church to sing "Jesus Loves Me." She also loves to visit her grandma's house, where she gets to play dress up in fancy clothes.

When Margaret isn't visiting with her three children and nine grandchildren, she enjoys reading the Bible, gardening, and bird watching. On September 9, Margaret and her husband William will celebrate their 55th wedding anniversary. Congratulations!

Margaret writes, "The Lord has been so good to us, and one of our blessings is receiving *Ideals*. We appreciate you honoring our Lord and His beautiful creation in each issue."

Thank you Dick Houghton and Margaret Weideman for sharing with *Ideals*. We hope to hear from other readers who would like to share photos and stories with the *Ideals* family. Please include a self-addressed, stamped envelope if you would like the photos returned. Keep your original photographs for safekeeping and send duplicate photos along with your name, address, and telephone number to:

Readers' Forum
Ideals Publications Inc.
P.O. Box 148000
Nashville, TN 37214-8000

What are friends for?

Tell your friends how much they mean to you by giving them Friendship Ideals. *After all, what are friends for?*

Order now and receive five copies of Friendship Ideals *for just $16.95 plus $3.50 postage and handling. That's a substantial savings over the newsstand price! Each magazine comes with a large greeting envelope to make your gift extra special.*

Order number 07808A

Send a check or money order payable to Ideals Publications Inc. to:

Ideals Friendship
P.O. Box 148000
Nashville, TN 37214-8000

Or call TOLL-FREE
1-800-558-4343
to place a credit card order.

Publisher, Patricia A. Pingry
Editor, Lisa C. Thompson
Art Director, Patrick McRae
Copy Editor, Laura Matter
Contributing Editors, Lansing Christman, Deana Deck, Russ Flint, Pamela Kennedy, Mary Skarmeas, Nancy Skarmeas

ACKNOWLEDGMENTS

A BOY AND HIS DOG from *WHEN DAY IS DONE* by Edgar Guest, copyright ©1921 by the Reilly & Lee Co., used by permission of the author's estate. SEPTEMBER GARDENS from *BEYOND THE RAINBOW* by Patience Strong, first published by Frederick Muller Ltd. in 1950, reproduced by permission of Rupert Crew Limited. THE INVISIBLE PLAYMATE from *LITTLE GIRL AND BOY LAND* by Margaret Widdemer, copyright 1924 by Harcourt Brace & Company and renewed 1952 by Margaret Widdemer Schauffler, reprinted by permission of the publisher. Our sincere thanks to the following authors whom we were unable to contact: Gladys Bussey for MEMORIES OF A GRADE SCHOOL TEACHER; Linda Emmons for HELLO, NEW FRIEND; Jennie Moulton for OLD TREASURES; Vida Poutz for MY FRIEND; Louise Weibert Sutton for FRIENDSHIP...BEST OF ALL; and William Arnette Wofford for SONG FOR OCTOBER.

New Friends & Old Friends

Joseph Parry

Make new friends, but keep the old;
Those are silver, these are gold.
New-made friendships, like new wine,
Age will mellow and refine.

Friendships that have stood the test—
Time and change—are surely best;
Brow may wrinkle, hair grow gray;
Friendship never knows decay.

For 'mid old friends, tried and true,
Once more we our youth renew.
But old friends, alas! may die;
New friends must their place supply.

Cherish friendship in your breast—
New is good, but old is best;
Make new friends but keep the old;
Those are silver, these are gold.